BLESSED

BLESSED

A Study of the Beatitudes

GWENDOLYN HARMON

Learning Ladyhood Press

Copyright © 2021 by Gwendolyn Harmon

All rights reserved. No part of this book may be reproduced in any manner whatsoever without written permission except in the case of brief quotations embodied in critical articles and reviews.

First Printing, 2021

Front cover photo by Rebecca Harmon, used with permission.
Back cover photo by Sherrilyn Shaw, used with permission.

Contents

Preface   1

PART 1
THE POOR IN SPIRIT

1   Beatitude #1: Poor in Spirit   4

2   Forgiven Much   8

PART 2
THEY THAT MOURN

3   Beatitude #2: They That Mourn   12

4   The Rejoicing Mourner and the Pouting Prophet   20

PART 3
THE MEEK

5   Beatitude # 3 The Meek   30

6   The Meekest Man and the Strongest Defender   37

PART 4
THEY THAT HUNGER AND THIRST AFTER RIGHTEOUSNESS

7   Beatitude #4: Hunger and Thirst after Righteousness   46

8	David's Hunger and Thirst for Righteousness	53

PART 5
THE MERCIFUL

9	Beatitude #5: The Merciful	60
10	The Merciful Stranger	65

PART 6
THE PURE IN HEART

11	Beatitude #6: Pure in Heart	70
12	Pure Heart in a Pagan Land	76

PART 7
THE PEACEMAKERS

13	Beatitude #7: Peacemakers	82
14	A Powerful Peacemaker	89

PART 8
PERSECUTED FOR RIGHTEOUSNESS

15	Beatitude #8 Persecuted	94
16	Blessed Are Ye	99

Preface

We all want God's blessing on our life. While we may long for it, and pray for it, and even fuss at God over it, the question to ask ourselves is: are we really willing to seek God's blessing *God's way*?

The Beatitudes are a passage of Scripture in which Jesus Himself literally tells us how to be people whom God can bless. He also describes what that blessing will look like. As we walk through this passage together, keep your eyes and heart open for how God is calling you to seek His blessing.

PART 1

The Poor in Spirit

I

Beatitude #1: Poor in Spirit

"Blessed are the poor in spirit, for theirs is the kingdom of heaven."(Matthew 5:3)

I remember reading this verse as a teen and wondering, *What does that mean?* I read the verse, I looked at the context, and I thought as hard as my teenaged reasoning capacity could manage, but to no avail. As I looked at this verse a couple of decades and two college degrees later, I took a more sophisticated approach: I looked up the words "poor" and "spirit" in my Strong's Concordance.

After scanning the list of other verses that use the same Greek words and looking up the definitions in the Greek dictionary at the back, I found that the words "poor" and "spirit" literally meant -drumroll, please- *poor* and *spirit*.

That's when I decided that *maybe* it was time to get some help from a couple of commentaries. I had some ideas about what the phrase might mean, but I wanted to make sure I was on the right track before I got too far.

I rummaged on my overstuffed bookshelves and came up with John Wesley and Matthew Henry, who confirmed my thoughts of what "poor in spirit" might mean. Here is how they described the poor in spirit:

> "The poor in spirit —they who are unfeignedly penitent, they who are truly convinced of sin; who see and feel the state they are in by nature, being deeply sensible of their sinfulness, guiltiness, helplessness." -John Wesley

> "These [the poor in spirit] bring their minds to their condition, when it is a low condition. They are humble and lowly in their own eyes. They see all their want, bewail their guilt, and thirst after a Redeemer."
> -Matthew Henry*

Poverty of spirit is essentially humility. In fact, it is necessary for salvation, for only the poor in spirit see their need of Christ's sacrifice as payment for their sin. To be poor in spirit is to have a repentant heart: a heart that agrees with God that it cannot measure up to God's standard of holiness —and that accepts God's holiness as the standard.

After salvation, it takes humility to *"walk worthy of God, who hath called you unto His kingdom and glory." (1 Thessalonians 2:12)*

And yet, just as Jesus promised, such humility is not without reward: 1 Peter 5:6 declares,

> "Humble yourselves therefore under the mighty hand of God,
> that He may exalt you in due time."

Jesus Christ, as God, willingly humbled Himself and lived as a man. He possessed all spiritual riches, and yet He chose to demonstrate His love by making Himself an example for the utterly destitute in spirit

(1 Peter 2:21.) And, just as 1 Peter 5:6 promises, God *did* exalt Jesus in due time. Philippians 2 says,

> "Wherefore God hath highly exalted Him, and given Him a name which is above every name" (v.9)

While we who really *are* poor in spirit *do* not and *could* not deserve the exaltation that belongs to Christ, God has chosen to exalt us despite our unworthiness. He exalts poor ransomed sinners far beyond what we could ever deserve, even making us *"joint-heirs with Christ."* (Romans 8:17)

I believe this is what Jesus is referring to when He says *"theirs is the kingdom of heaven."* As joint-heirs, we will inherit a portion of the kingdom of heaven *with Christ*.

Our position as heirs is due to the fact that when we trust Christ for salvation, God the Father adopts us as His own children. Romans 8:15-17 says,

> "For ye have not received the spirit of bondage again to fear; but ye have received the Spirit of adoption, whereby we cry, Abba, Father. The Spirit itself beareth witness with our spirit, that we are the children of God: and if children, then heirs; heirs of God, and joint-heirs with Christ; if so be that we suffer with Him, that we may be also glorified together."

Another passage that describes this truth is Galatians 4:5-7, which says that Christ came,

> "To redeem them that were under the law, that we might receive the adoption of sons. And because ye are sons, God hath sent forth the Spirit of His Son into your hearts, crying, Abba, Father. Wherefore thou art no more a servant, but a son; and if a son, then an heir of God through Christ."

The wonderful gift of salvation is not only to allow us to escape from sin's penalty. It is to raise us from our poverty and welcome us into a family, a home, and an inheritance beyond anything we could ever dream possible.

And it is all of His mercy, which He freely lavished on us, knowing how undeserving we truly are. Titus illustrates this wonderfully:

"For we ourselves also were sometimes foolish, disobedient, deceived, serving divers lusts and pleasures, living in malice and envy, hateful, and hating one another. But after that the kindness and love of God our Saviour toward man appeared, Not by works of righteousness which we have done, but according to His mercy He saved us, by the washing of regeneration, and renewing of the Holy Ghost; Which He shed on us abundantly through Jesus Christ our Saviour; That being justified by His grace, we should be made heirs according to the hope of eternal life." (3:3-7)

When we set our hearts to seek God, we are demonstrating that "poor in spirit" humility which acknowledges our need for God, whether for salvation or for sanctification. The poor in spirit yield to God because they see their own inadequacy to live life apart from His presence and help, and receive in return an inheritance the Bible describes as *"incorruptible, and undefiled, and that fadeth not away, reserved in heaven for you."* (1 Peter 1:4)

*Parallel Commentary on the New Testament. (Chattanooga: AMG Publishers 2003) p.12-13

2

Forgiven Much

Luke 7:36-50

A Pharisee named Simon invited Jesus to eat with him. When they had sat down, reclining at the table as the custom was, a woman entered. She held an alabaster box of ointment in her hands as she made her way to Jesus' feet. Weeping, she washed His feet with her tears, dried them with her hair, and reverently kissed His feet as she poured the ointment on them. Observing this spectacle, Simon thought to himself,

"This Man, if He were a prophet, would have known who and what manner of woman this is that toucheth Him: for she is a sinner." (Luke 7:39)

The woman was evidently known for her sin, whatever it may have been, and Simon certainly viewed this woman as an outcast. But Jesus knew what the Pharisee was thinking. Imagine the scene as you read the following conversation:

"Simon, I have somewhat to say unto thee.

And he saith, Master, say on.

There was a certain creditor which had two debtors: the one owed five hundred pence, and the other fifty. And when they had nothing to pay, he frankly forgave them both. Tell me therefore, which of them will love him most?

Simon answered and said, I suppose that he, to whom he forgave most.

And He said unto him, Thou hast rightly judged. And He turned to the woman, and said unto Simon, Seest Thou this woman? I entered into thine house, thou gavest Me no water for my feet: but she hath washed my feet with tears, and wiped them with the hairs of her head. Thou gavest Me no kiss, but this woman since the time I came in hath not ceased to kiss My feet. My head with oil thou didst not anoint: but this woman hath anointed my feet with ointment. Wherefore I say unto thee, Her sins, which are many, are forgiven; for she loved much: but to whom little is forgiven, the same loveth little." (Luke 7:40-47)

Jesus took the opportunity to teach Simon (and the other people present) about the connection between love and forgiveness. The woman was "poor in spirit," weeping over her sin while demonstrating her love for the One who had forgiven her.

The woman's sinful past caused other sinners to reject her, but when she turned to the sinless Christ in repentance and faith, He welcomed her freely, saying, *"Thy sins are forgiven."* (Luke 7:48)

Her love welled up out of her poverty of spirit, that humility that sees sin as God sees it: wretched, offensive, and inexcusable apart from Christ's blood. Because she knew the magnitude of her debt, the magnitude of Christ's forgiveness inspired the woman to greater love.

In the same way, our love for God often serves as an indication of our humility. A humble heart will see just how much Christ has done on its behalf, but a prideful heart will be cold toward God, underestimating or undervaluing His forgiveness. True love will always lead to actions. Where we love deeply, we are willing to sacrifice deeply for the sake of the beloved. The way we live our lives will always display our love for God.

However, just as the Pharisees did in Jesus' day, it can be easy to think that actions are the goal: that if we have the right actions we *must* have right hearts before the Lord. It is equally easy to dismiss the outward display of our love for God because of the hypocrisy of those who take the Pharisee's view and emphasize actions alone.

Both views are unbiblical, because, while it is possible to have right actions without a right heart, a right heart will always show itself in right actions. *(Matthew 7:16-20)*

Now, dear reader, have you been forgiven? How well does your love demonstrate the enormity of the forgiveness Christ has given you?

PART 2

They That Mourn

3

Beatitude #2: They That Mourn

"Blessed are they that mourn: for they shall be comforted."
(Matthew 5:4)

This beatitude always seemed to me as if it painted a rather bleak picture of Christianity. To go through life mourning seems the opposite of Christ's statement that He came so we might have joy. *(John 15:11)* But these also are the words of Christ in Matthew 5, calling those who mourn *blessed*.

The word *mourn* used here means to grieve or wail. But what is it we are to grieve over? There are two times recorded in Scripture when Jesus Himself wept, and two more occasions when it is said He was sorrowful over something. As Christians, we are followers of Christ, *(1 Peter 2:21)* so it seems appropriate to ask ourselves what Christ mourned over?

The Consequences of Sin

Palm branches waved in the air, people shouted and ran and tore branches off the trees to cast on the road. Hosannas filled the air as Jesus made His way to Jerusalem on a donkey, fulfilling prophecy that declared Him to be the long-awaited Messiah. But in the midst of all the rejoicing and jubilation of His triumphal entry, Jesus stopped and did what would seem to us a very strange thing.

"And when He was come near, He beheld the city, and wept over it, Saying, If thou hadst known, even thou, at least in this thy day, the things which belong unto thy peace! But now they are hid from thine eyes. For the days shall come upon thee, that thine enemies shall cast a trench about thee, and compass thee round, and keep thee on every side, And shall lay thee even with the ground, and thy children within thee; and they shall not leave in thee one stone upon another; because thou knewest not the time of thy visitation." (Luke 19:41-44)

Jesus mourned over the destruction Israel's sin would bring upon the city and its inhabitants. He mourned over their coming rejection of the Messiah they had waited for so long. Having no sin of His own to mourn, He mourned over the sins of others and the devastation which they had willingly chosen.

Jesus lamented over Jerusalem and its inhabitants another time also, saying,

"O Jerusalem, Jerusalem, thou that killest the prophets, and stonest them which are sent unto thee, how often would I have gathered thy children together, even as a hen gathereth her chickens under her wings, and ye would not." (Matthew 23:37)

This outpouring of heart shows that Jesus longed for His people to repent. He mourned over their rebellion against God, grieved over their sin, but desired to restore them nevertheless.

They had rejected God time and again, persecuting the prophets whom He had sent to warn and rebuke them. Jesus knew they would soon reject Him once and for all with the same zeal with which they had persecuted the prophets, and yet He wept over the destruction of their city.

He wept over the people of Jerusalem and the devastation they would endure, even though that devastation was the just result of their choice to reject God and go their own way.

This demonstrates the truth that a God-ward heart will mourn over souls still unrepentant towards God. It will also sorrow over those who have rejected or wronged us with a heart yearning to forgive and to restore –just as God has forgiven and restored us.

The Sorrows of Others

It is written of Jesus many times in the Gospels that "He had compassion" on individuals and on groups of people. His compassion led Him to provide food for a multitude, heal the sick, give sight to the blind, touch lepers (to heal them,) teach the multitudes, and raise the dead. In fact, many if not most of the miracles done by Jesus were directly stated to have been motivated by compassion. But Jesus also showed compassion another way.

On one occasion, Jesus had a friend named Lazarus, who died. There is much I could say about the details of this event, but to summarize, Jesus knew His friend was sick and had chosen to wait until after Lazarus had died to travel to Bethany, where Lazarus and his sisters lived.

When Jesus arrived, Lazarus' sisters each came out to speak with Him, and both voiced the same thought:

"Lord, if Thou hadst been here, my brother had not died." (John 11:21,32)

Lazarus' sister Martha notably followed this thought up with,

"But I know, that, even now, whatsoever Thou wilt ask of God, God will give it Thee." (v.22)

This statement of Martha's prompted the beautiful words of Jesus, in which He declared Himself to be the Resurrection and the Life. However, when Mary came and spoke the same initial thought to Him, falling down at His feet and weeping, this is what John records:

"When Jesus therefore saw her weeping, and the Jews also weeping which came with her, He groaned in the Spirit and was troubled, And said, Where have ye laid him? They said unto Him, Lord, come and see." (vv. 33-34)

Then comes that famous verse, the shortest verse in the Bible, but which speaks such volumes:

"Jesus wept."

Jesus *knew* He would raise Lazarus from the dead. He *knew* that Lazarus' resurrection had been His and the Father's purpose all along, and yet in the face of such sorrow, Jesus wept.

One could argue, and many have, that He was weeping over the consequences of sin on the human race at large, but look at the context again: He *saw* those specific people who were weeping, and then He wept with them. This reminds me of Romans 12:15, which tells us to

"Rejoice with them that do rejoice, and weep with them that weep."

Jesus demonstrated the kind of compassion that willingly enters into the sorrow of others, mourning because they mourn, even while confident that God is able and willing to comfort them. That brings us to Jesus' next point. Blessed are they that mourn, but why?

"For they shall be comforted."

Herein lies the blessedness, the joy behind the mourning. The word *comfort* comes from the same root word as the word Jesus uses in John 14: 16-18 in reference to the Holy Spirit:

"And I will pray the Father, and He shall give you another Comforter, that He may abide with you for ever; Even the Spirit of truth; whom the world cannot receive, because it seeth Him not, neither knoweth him: but ye know Him; for He dwelleth with you, and shall be in you. I will not leave you comfortless: I will come to you."

One of the key purposes of the indwelling of the Holy Spirit is to comfort us. Why would God care so much about our comfort? 2 Corinthians 1: 3-5 gives the answer.

"Blessed be God, even the Father of our Lord Jesus Christ, the Father of mercies, and the God of all comfort" (v.3)

First of all, God cares to comfort us because He is merciful. He is *"the Father of mercies."* He is capable of comforting us, because He is *"the God of all comfort."* But there's more to this business of comforting:

"Who comforteth us in all our tribulation, that we may be able to comfort them which are in any trouble, by the comfort wherewith we ourselves are comforted of God." (v.4)

You see, there's a greater purpose in view than just our own comfort. God in His mercy comforts us, but in His wisdom, He does it in such a way that *we* can then be part of that comforting process in the life of a fellow believer *because* of the suffering that caused us to need comforting in the first place. If that isn't an example of Romans 8:28 at work, I'm not sure what is!

And that's not all:

> *"For as the sufferings of Christ abound in us,*
> *so our consolation also aboundeth by Christ." (v. 5)*

The more we suffer, or, in the context of our present study, the more we mourn, the more we are comforted! God never runs out of comfort. It is always abundant, always there to draw upon when we need it.

Jesus says we are blessed to mourn because there is a certainty that we *will* receive comfort. Yet despite the glorious truth that God Himself is our Comforter, we may still be inclined to feel that even Divine comfort does not make up for the pain and sorrow of a mournful time. But Jesus knows us. To help us with our perspective, He chose to include in Luke a parallel passage to the beatitudes, in which He reverses the concepts of Matthew 5 to show us the eternal perspective behind them.

"But woe unto you that are rich! For ye have received your consolation. Woe unto you that are full! For ye shall hunger. Woe unto you that laugh now! For ye shall mourn and weep." (Luke 6:24-25)

And again elsewhere, Jesus says,

> *"Verily, verily, I say unto you, That ye shall weep and lament, but the world shall rejoice: and ye shall be sorrowful, but your sorrow shall be turned into joy." (John 16:20)*

The world around us may *seem* happier on the surface, but the truth is, that happiness is not only superficial: it is also temporal. The Christian may mourn more, but even in the midst of that mourning, God can give joy. Matthew Henry describes it this way:

> *"As in vain and sinful laughter the heart is sorrowful, so in gracious mourning the heart has a serious joy, a secret satisfaction, which a stranger does not intermeddle with."**

Just as the world may laugh on the outside while empty on the inside, a Christian will mourn from the heart, but in that heart have the quiet joy and peace of knowing the mourning is but for a season, and that comfort is at hand.

On the other hand, those who never mourn over their sin in *this* life will have ample cause to mourn over it throughout eternity to come. As 2 Corinthians 7:10 reminds us,

> *"godly sorrow worketh repentance to salvation not to be repented of: but the sorrow of the world worketh death."*

Solomon wrote,

> *"It is better to go to the house of mourning, than to go to the house of feasting: for that is the end of all men; and the living will lay it to his heart."*
> (Ecclesiastes 7:2)

The place of mourning sets our focus on eternal things. It helps us follow the command of Colossians 3:2, which tells us to

> *"Set your affection on things above, not on things on the earth."*

Are you willing to follow the God of all comfort through the valley of mourning, or are you chasing after the superficial comforts of the world?

*Matthew Henry: *Commentary on the Bible* (Grand Rapids: The Zondervan Corporation 1960) p. 1220

4

The Rejoicing Mourner and the Pouting Prophet

Mourning is meant to be a part of the Christian life. When our hearts are in tune with the heart of God, we *will* mourn: over our own sin, over the sins of others, and in sympathy with others who are mourning. Yet, Jesus *did* say, "These things have I spoken unto you, that My joy might remain in you, and that your joy might be full." (John 15:11)

How do we reconcile the two statements? I think a quick overview of the life of Paul can help:

The Rejoicing Mourner

Acts 7 ends with a tumult of activity. Stephen has just finished presenting Jesus as the culmination of long ages of waiting for the promised Messiah. The council was in uproar, enraged at his teaching, when Stephen suddenly looked up, saying,

"Behold, I see the heavens opened, and the Son of man standing on the right hand of God." (v.56)

That was the final straw for the council, who then rushed Stephen out to be executed.

But in all the rush and tumult, there was an island: a young man named Saul stood by watching, approving, and perhaps even longing to participate. The men cast their coats at his feet so they could aim their stones better, and Saul stood still, guarding their garments. Even Stephen's cry of *"Lord, lay not this sin to their charge"* (v.60) could not move his stony heart.

Scripture tells us that Saul not only approved of Stephen's execution, but himself began actively hunting down any Christian he could find. Young, old, man, woman, all Christians were alike to him: rebels, heretics, in need of being rooted out and exterminated.

But then...

Acts 9 returns to Saul's narrative, telling how he went to the high priest, *"breathing out threatenings and slaughter against the disciples of the Lord"*(v.1) and asked for letters to the synagogues of Damascus which would permit him to ferret out Christians wherever he went, taking them prisoners to be brought back to Jerusalem.

On the way to Damascus, however, a wondrous thing occurred. Saul literally *met* Jesus and was instantly changed. Gone was his hatred of Christians –he now was one himself!

Scripture does not tell us why or how or even exactly when, but Saul underwent a name change and began to go by the name of Paul. It is by this name Christians are most familiar with him. It was Paul who authored many of the books of the New Testament.

It was Paul who set off on those now-famous missionary journeys to proclaim the gospel to the Gentiles. It was Paul who wrote letters to young preachers Timothy and Titus, and it was Paul whom God used to spread the gospel of Christ and disciple churches like no one else mentioned in Scripture. What a change!

But Paul's past didn't just disappear. When he first became a Christian, no one believed it. Instead of being welcomed into the fellowship of believers with all the excitement of a soul added to the church, Paul was kept at a distance and viewed with suspicion and fear.

This continued until a man named Barnabas came alongside Paul. He believed Paul's story of his conversion and personally introduced him to fellow believers who otherwise would have been afraid to take a chance on this man who until recently had considered himself their enemy.

We know Paul certainly never forgot the sins of his past. In 1 Corinthians 15:9, he says,

> "For I am the least of the apostles, that am not meet to be called an apostle, because I persecuted the church of God."

But did Paul ever *mourn* over his sin? Romans 7 gives us the answer:

> "I find then a law, that, when I would do good, evil is present with me. For I delight in the law of God after the inward man: But I see another law in my members, warring against the law of my mind, and bringing me into captivity to the law of sin which is in my members.
> O wretched man that I am! Who shall deliver me from the body of this death?" (vv.21-25)

Paul mourned, not just over the sin of his past, but over the sins he found himself committing even after salvation. In fact, from this passage and others, I get the impression that Paul's mourning was more focused on his *ongoing* battle with sin.

You see, when we are saved, we are delivered from the power of sin. We are made free to obey God and do what is right, but we are not forced to do so. Because our bodies still carry around our old sin nature, we wrestle, as Paul did, with the opposing pulls of sin and righteousness. We often want to do both, but we have to choose one, and quite often we do not choose righteousness.

That is what Paul is mourning in this passage. He wants to do right, and yet he does wrong. He cannot get away from his own sinful flesh, and he cries out in despair,

"O wretched man that I am! Who shall deliver me from the body of this death?"

But then, after the swelling cry of agony expressed in that final question, there is the joy of the answer:

"I thank God through Jesus Christ our Lord. So then with the mind I myself serve the law of God but with the flesh the law of sin. There is therefore now no condemnation to them which are in Christ Jesus, who walk not after the flesh, but after the Spirit. For the law of the Spirit of life in Christ Jesus hath made me free from the law of sin and death." (7:25-8:2)

Who shall deliver us from sin? All the fulness of the Godhead working in concert on our behalf! That is the rejoicing to which our mourning leads us.

Our mourning also leads us to enter into the heart of God for others. Later in Romans, Paul writes,

> "Brethren, my heart's desire and prayer to God for Israel is, that they might be saved." (10:1)

The remarkable thing about this is that these same Jews of Israel for whom Paul prayed were the very ones persecuting Paul and the other Christians. The book of Acts records how the Jews in different cities reviled, maligned, injured, tortured, even attempted to kill Paul, and yet he had such a burden for their salvation! In fact, he was even able to sincerely say,

> "I have great heaviness and continual sorrow in my heart. For I could wish that myself were accursed from Christ for my brethren, my kinsmen according to the flesh." (Romans 9:2-3)

He knew it was not possible for him to forfeit his own salvation and give it instead to the Jews, but that was his heart: he desired their salvation even to the point of wishing he could go to hell in their place. To Paul, even eternal torment was not too much to endure if it meant that those Jews who were persecuting him could be saved.

The Pouting Prophet

The heart of the mourner is a heart of compassion. When we cease to mourn over our sin, we lose our heart of compassion towards others.

The book of Jonah gives us an example of a man who neglected to see his sin as God saw it, and what effect that had on his compassion for others.

The story of Jonah is well known. He is the prophet who spent three days in the belly of a large fish because he ran from God. But let's go a little deeper than the Sunday-school lesson and focus in on Jonah's view of sin, both his own and that of the Ninevites.

When asked to take a message of impending judgment to his people's worst enemies, Jonah ran away, knowing that God is merciful and would forgive them if they repented. After tossing in a storm that scared even the seasoned sailors on his ship and eventually being thrown overboard and swallowed by a Divinely-prepared fish, Jonah finally prayed to God with at least some measure of repentance, saying,

> "But I will sacrifice unto Thee with the voice of thanksgiving; I will pay that that I have vowed. Salvation is of the Lord." (2:9)

God spoke to the fish, which then spewed Jonah up on dry land.

Then Jonah is again commanded to go to Ninevah, and as I read the account of Jonah's proclamation to the people, I can almost see him, dragging his feet and saying in the flattest monotone, perhaps even mumbling,

> *"Yet forty days, and Nineveh shall be overthrown."* (3:4)

He certainly seems to have been half-hearted in his mission, because the city was three days' journey across, and he only went in about a day's journey. There did not seem to be any concern on his part everyone in the city hear the important message of God's judgment.

Yet, after Jonah's message was delivered, the whole city repented (beginning with the king!) and God showed mercy. Jonah, instead of being pleased with the change in Nineveh's hearts, prayed angrily to God with a definite I-told-you-so attitude, complaining about God's mercy on this wicked people.

After that, he stormed out of the city and settled into a makeshift shelter on the hillside to see if God would change His mind and destroy the people anyway.

You see, Jonah knew how to mourn, but his mourning was all about himself.

God, in an amazing display of mercy and patient love, didn't just leave Jonah on the hillside to waste away while he waited in vain for God's judgment to fall. Instead, he arranged for an illustration of Jonah's misplaced mourning.

God caused a plant to grow, providing shade for Jonah as he pouted on the hillside, which Jonah thoroughly enjoyed. The next day, God sent a worm to eat the plant. This made Jonah angry, and he again complained to God, who replied by pointing out Jonah's lack of compassion:

"Thou hast had pity on the gourd, for the which thou hast not laboured, neither madest it grow; which came up in a night, and perished in a night: And should not I spare Nineveh, that great city, wherein are more than sixscore thousand persons that cannot discern between their right hand and their left hand; and also much cattle?" (4:10-11)

Jonah was wrapped up in his disgust and hatred of the sins of Nineveh, (which were many,) but had no sense of his own sinful attitudes and actions.

The people of Nineveh were born in a pagan society, steeped in idol worship. They would not have had the privilege of being taught God's Word. They were as wicked as one might expect a pagan people to be, but what was Jonah's excuse?

The Assyrians who inhabited Nineveh were infamous for their unspeakable cruelty towards their conquered enemies; but there on the hillside was Jonah, himself wishing complete and utter destruction upon the entire city with as much hatred and anger as the Assyrians had ever displayed.

The Ninevites were idolaters, it was true, but Jonah had literally just *run away* from God.

His refusal to obey showed that his own idea of right was more important to him than obedience to God. So in a sense, Jonah's sinful attitudes and decisions were just as "bad" as those of Nineveh –if not worse.

In God's eyes, Jonah was as much a sinner as the Ninevites were. Jonah himself had deserved divine judgment for his sins, and yet he had no compassion for them. He was like the man in the parable who begged to be forgiven of a debt he could not pay, then turned around and threw someone who owed *him* money into prison, instead of extending the mercy his creditor had shown in forgiving his debt. (Matthew 18:23-35)

Could it be that Jonah had forgotten to mourn over his sin? Could he have gotten comfortable with excusing in *himself* the very cruelty he despised in his enemies?

Sometimes, you and I can be just like Jonah. When we neglect prayer or rush past the part where we confess our sins to God, we quickly become self-focused and self-righteous. Our compassion weakens with every excuse, with every pricking of our conscience that we push aside.

Only when we see our sin as it is in the eyes of God and acknowledge our ever-present poverty of spirit will we mourn over our sins, which are the very sins Christ died to pay for.

As we mourn, we receive the comfort and joy of forgiveness, which in turn helps us see others as Christ sees them: as sinners in need of the Savior. That is where true compassion comes from.

Titus 3:3-7 says,

"For we ourselves also were sometimes foolish, disobedient, deceived, serving divers lusts and pleasures, living in malice and envy, hateful, and hating one another. But after that the kindness and love of God our Saviour toward man appeared, Not by works of righteousness which we have done, but according to His mercy He saved us, by the washing of regeneration, and renewing of the Holy Ghost; Which He shed on us abundantly through Jesus Christ our Saviour; That being justified by His grace, we should be made heirs according to the hope of eternal life."

We were once in the same lost state as those whose wickedness so offends us now. The proper view of what Christ has forgiven in us will inspire compassion for a lost and dying world. A lack of compassion shows us that we need to stop and remember our own sin, to mourn over it, asking God to forgive our pride and give us a heart for those He loves.

PART 3

The Meek

5

Beatitude # 3 The Meek

"Blessed are the meek: for they shall inherit the earth."
(Matthew 5:5)

What do you think of when you hear someone described as *meek*? Do you envision someone with a mousey personality, easily led, indecisive, or weak? That is how society tends to view meekness, but what is it really?

Meekness Defined

The Greek word used by Jesus means mild or humble. It is essentially the same Greek word Jesus uses to describe Himself in Matthew 11:29 when He says,

> *"Take My yoke upon you, and learn of Me; for I am meek and lowly in heart: and ye shall find rest unto your souls."*

Meekness, then, is an attribute of God Himself. Matthew Henry puts it this way:

> "They are the meek, who would rather forgive twenty injuries than revenge one."*

And isn't that just what Jesus did? On the cross, He looked at His torturers and said,

> "Father, forgive them; for they know not what they do." (Luke 23:34)

2 Corinthians 5:21 tells us,

> "For He hath made Him to be sin for us, who knew no sin; that we might be made the righteousness of God in Him."

God had every right to heap upon us the eternal punishment our sin so justly deserves; but instead, He chose to suffer *Himself* so that we might be offered forgiveness.

John Wesley describes the meek as,

> "They that hold all their passions and affections evenly balanced."**

This, too, is a hallmark of the attributes of God: they are always perfectly in balance. Never does God's justice overrun His mercy, nor will His love overpower His holiness. All these things work together in perfect harmony. Every aspect of God's nature works together, providing us with a perfect picture of meekness.

Another way to understand meekness is as "power under control," which, according to Warren Wiersbe, is how the Greeks would have understood the word used in Matthew 5:3. The word was often used to describe a horse that had been broken: still as powerful as ever, only now brought under the control of the rider. ***

When we are meek, we are brought under the control of the Holy Spirit. Jesus is, of course, the best example of this. He was fully God, yet fully man, and as our example, He submitted Himself entirely to the authority of the Father. As He says in John 8:29,

> *"And He that sent Me is with Me: the Father hath not left Me alone; for I do always those things that please Him."*

Paul urges us to set our focus on pleasing God in 2 Timothy 2:4.

> *"No man that warreth entangleth himself with the affairs of this life; that he may please him who hath chosen him to be a soldier."*

Just as a good soldier will bring his physical, mental, and emotional strength under the control of his commanding officer, so we bring all our strength (and our weaknesses, too) under the control of the Holy Spirit.

Meekness Defended

That God values meekness is evident from a quick glance through the verses containing the word "meekness" in both the Old and New Testaments. Here is just a sampling from the Old Testament:

> "The meek shall eat and be satisfied: they shall praise the Lord that seek Him: your heart shall live for ever." Psalm 22:26

> "The meek will He guide in judgment: and the meek will He teach His way." Psalm 25:9

> "But the meek shall inherit the earth; and shall delight themselves in the abundance of peace." Psalm 37:11

> "The Lord lifteth up the meek: He casteth down the wicked down to the ground." Psalm 147:6

> "For the Lord taketh pleasure in His people: He will beautify the meek with salvation." Psalm 149:4

> "The meek also shall increase their joy in the Lord, and the poor among men shall rejoice in the Holy One of Israel." Isaiah 29:19

There are a few things that stand out to me from these verses. The first is that the meek will have a trusting contentment in all that God allows. They *"shall eat and be satisfied" (Psalm 22:26)*, they will rejoice in God *(Isaiah 29:19)*, characterized by joy that increases more and more as they continue to seek God.

The second thing that I noticed about the meek in the verses above is that God is their Defender. Our society often likes to portray the meek as victims, and champions those who demand, defend, and make themselves obnoxious as they agitate for what they perceive to be their "rights."

These are the ones our society looks up to and strives to emulate, but for the Christian, a life of meekness is not a life of being victimized: our Defender is all-knowing, all-powerful, and loves us deeply.

The heart that chooses to respond to life in meekness is something that God both values and protects. A good example of this is found in 1 Peter 3:4, which tells us that women should be adorned with

> *"the ornament of a meek and quiet spirit,*
> *which is in the sight of God of great price."*

I don't know about you, but to think that anything pertaining to *me* could be "of great price" in the eyes of God is absolutely stunning. It is a sad commentary on modern Christianity that Christian women don't strive after or even value a meek and quiet spirit as we should.

In our feminist culture, the bare mention of the words "meek" and "quiet" is sure to offend, even in Christian circles. Yet, if God so values meekness and quietness in us, should we not value it also?

Meekness and quietness go hand-in-hand with contentment. When our hearts are trusting in God, we will be secure in His Person and provision; and we will live our lives in simple contentment. And Christian contentment does not clamor over offenses, small or great, nor does it demand its due: it has the faith to let God defend.

This runs against our nature, and the lies of the world may have crept far enough into our minds that this idea of meekness as a virtue seems completely foreign. Push your initial reaction aside, however, and look instead at Christ, who is our ultimate standard of what is good and true.

"For even hereunto were ye called: because Christ also suffered for us, leaving us an example, that ye should follow His steps: Who did no sin, neither was guile found in His mouth: Who, when He was reviled, reviled not again; when He suffered, He threatened not; but committed Himself to Him that judgeth righteously: Who His own self bare our sins in His own body on the tree, that we, being dead to sins, should live unto righteousness: by whose stripes ye were healed." (1 Peter 2:21-24)

Inheriting the Earth

Jesus says that the meek shall inherit the earth. This is almost a direct quote of Psalm 37:11, which says,

> *"But the meek shall inherit the earth; and shall delight themselves in the abundance of peace."*

The thought of Israel possessing and passing on their God-given land is a thread that runs throughout the Bible. These words, spoken to a Jewish audience languishing under Roman rule, may have been a radical blow to their idea of what the Messiah would accomplish, and how it would be done.

The Jewish people had expected that the Messiah would kick out the Romans, defeating them with military might, but Jesus said that the earth, or land, would be inherited by the meek, not the warrior.

From the context of this beatitude, it is difficult to tell whether Christ is referring to the specific land of Israel, the whole present earth, or the new earth to come. In fact, the same Greek word for *earth* here is used elsewhere in Scripture to refer to each of those things.

But regardless of whether Jesus is referring to the present earth or the new earth, I am certain that the meek will delight in their inheritance, for they will be fully content to enjoy whatever God's goodness bestows upon them.

We could easily get bogged down in speculations of who and what and when, but we must be careful not to miss the truth being expressed. The point Christ is making is that the kingdom of God is not to be won or defended with military might or physical strength, but rather soul by soul, through the power of the Gospel at work through the meekness of its messengers.

*Matthew Henry: *Commentary on the Bible* (Grand Rapids: The Zondervan Corporation 1960) 1220

**John Wesley: *Parallel Commentary on the New Testament.* (Chattanooga: AMG Publishers 2003) 14

***Warren Wiersbe, *The Bible Exposition Commentary* (Colorado Springs: Victor Books 200) 21

6

The Meekest Man and the Strongest Defender

Apart from the example of Jesus Himself, the best example in the Bible of meekness is seen in the book of Numbers, where Moses is described as

> *"very meek, above all the men which were upon the face of the earth."*
> *(12:3)*

This remarkable statement is sandwiched between two events that put Moses' meekness on display. In Numbers 11, the Israelites complained about the food God had provided. Moses, frustrated with the people's grumbling, began to complain to God about the heavy burden the people had become.

God had mercy on Moses and told him to gather 70 men out of the elders of Israel to take some of the heavy load of responsibility Moses had been bearing. They were to gather around the tabernacle, where God would give them His Spirit.

When the men gathered, however, two were missing. For whatever reason, they had decided to stay in camp instead of following God's instructions by going to the tabernacle. When God put His Spirit on the rest of the men, they began to prophesy –as did the two who stayed behind.

When Joshua heard about this, He said to Moses,

> "My lord Moses, forbid them." (v. 28)

I love Moses' response:

> "Enviest thou for my sake? would God that all the Lord's people were prophets, and that the Lord would put His spirit upon them!" (v. 29)

You see, Moses wasn't concerned about hoarding the authority or power given to him by God. Instead of jealously guarding his position as the only one chosen by God to lead the people, he was glad to see others serving God and being directed by the Holy Spirit.

Part of meekness is being satisfied with the position, place, or type of service God has given you. It also means staying close to God in trusting contentment when He allows others to "encroach" upon the areas of ministry or ability which we view as our territory.

We might have been tempted to side with Joshua if we had been in Moses' place. The natural reaction of our flesh is to become jealous or defensive when others are promoted or made much of, but Moses freely supported these men upon whom God had put His Spirit.

The fleshly response is exhibited again later in this passage, for while Moses took this sharing of authority as from the Lord, Aaron and Miriam chose instead to take offense.

Their initial complaint against Moses was personal, (regarding his choice of wife,) but notice what their argument against him really was:

> "Hath the Lord indeed spoken only by Moses?
> Hath He not spoken also by us?" (12:2)

Note their attempt to claim a position of equal authority and importance with Moses. God chose not to record any of the words they spoke against Moses' wife, but preserved forever the two short sentences that reveal the heart behind their attack on God's chosen leader.

Perhaps they were jealous that they had not been given a position among the newly appointed leaders, perhaps they were offended by the fact that God had *Moses* choose the 70, or perhaps it was a simple case of grownup sibling rivalry: whatever their reasons may have been, *God* took note of their disrespect and presumption.

> "And the Lord heard it." (12:2)

This is the point at which we are given the parenthetical statement about Moses being the meekest man on earth. I think God placed that there because He wanted us to sit up and take notice of what He was going to do on Moses' behalf.

By inserting the statement, God takes us out of the narrative for a moment, prompting us to read on with renewed focus. It also brings to our attention the particular quality God wants us to notice about Moses in this account.

Before we go on to look at what God does in defense of Moses, I want to point out that simple statement, *"And the Lord heard it."*

Whatever false accusations, gossip, rumors, or spiteful words may be spoken against us, we can be sure that God hears them all. He is not only omniscient, but also omnipresent, and there is nothing which escapes His notice.

We have no record of Moses speaking even a word in his own defense. Matthew Henry points out,

> "When God's honour was concerned, as in the case of the golden calf, no man more zealous than Moses; but, when his own honour was touched, no man more meek: as bold as a lion in the cause of God, but as mild as a lamb in his own cause."*

As the two took Moses to task, God stepped in:

"And the Lord spake suddenly unto Moses, and unto Aaron, and unto Miriam, Come out ye three unto the tabernacle of the congregation. And they three came out. And the Lord came down in the pillar of the cloud, and stood in the door of the tabernacle, and called Aaron and Miriam: and they both came forth. And He said, Hear now My words: If there be a prophet among you, I the Lord will make Myself known unto him in a vision, and will speak unto him in a dream. My servant Moses is not so, who is faithful in all Mine house. With him will I speak mouth to mouth, even apparently, and not in dark speeches; and the similitude of the Lord shall he behold: wherefore then were ye not afraid to speak against My servant Moses?" (vv.4-8)

God Himself defends Moses far more successfully than any attempt on Moses' part could have done. In asserting both Moses' importance and his authority, God confirms his worthiness for his position, declaring that Moses *"is faithful in all Mine house."*

God also highlights the difference in His relationship with Moses, removing the last possible objection they might have regarding Moses' position as leader of Israel.

Upon this declaration in Moses' defense, the cloud departs, and Miriam is left leprous. One commentary I read pointed out that Aaron, as High Priest, would have been the judge in cases of leprosy, and as such would have been the one responsible to pronounce upon his sister the sentence of "unclean," knowing all the while that his own sin had been just as severe as hers.

Characteristically, Aaron rushed to apologize, asking Moses to intercede on Miriam's behalf. Moses prayed, without a shadow of malice or bitterness towards the siblings who had been railing against him just minutes before.

Striking the Rock

Moses met this wave of malice with victorious meekness, but although he was the meekest man on the earth, he was not perfect. Scripture also records for us a time when Moses failed to respond in meekness.

In Numbers 20, Moses and the people are wandering in the desert, having rejected the promised land in unbelief. The people then display further unbelief by raising a typical panic-stricken cry of complaint: they needed water...and they needed it *now*. And of course, as they typically did, they blamed Moses, accusing him of bringing them into the wilderness to die.

Moses took their complaint to God, and God gave Moses some very clear instructions as to how He will provide water for the people. (It is important to note that this was not the first time God provided water for the people.)

Moses went before the people, but though God had instructed him to speak to the rock, which would then produce water, Moses lost his temper and spoke instead *to the people.*

That in itself was not the problem: it was what he said that shows a lack of meekness.

"And Moses and Aaron gathered the congregation together before the rock, and he said unto them, Hear now, ye rebels; must we fetch you water out of this rock?" (Numbers 20:10)

Just as Miriam and Aaron had tried to make themselves seem like they were equal in authority with Moses, so Moses here commits the grave transgression of making himself seem equal with God Himself. Miriam and Aaron's statement had been prideful, but Moses' claim is downright blasphemous! As if his help was in any way needed for God to bring water out of the rock! On top of this, he struck the rock instead of speaking to it, which was disobedience to God's clear instructions.

Notice that Moses struck the rock *twice.* Apparently, nothing happened the first time. What a sickening moment that must have been for all concerned! It was the first time the people had ever seen Moses fail to produce what he had said he would while representing God to them.

Consider the mercy of God: the second time Moses struck the rock, water came out! God could have left Moses high and dry –literally! But instead, He showed His power and His mercy by confirming Moses' words to the people that He would supply water. This double attempt did, however, show that *God* was the One providing water, not Moses.

You can read about the judgment God laid upon Moses for his pride and disobedience in the verses which follow our passage, but my point here is to give a contrast, an example of both the right and wrong ways to respond to spiteful untruths. This account also reminds us that no one is immune from falling into sin, even in the area in which their character is the strongest.

From these accounts we can glean a vital truth about God: He calls us to meekness fully intending to defend us Himself.

Meekness means letting go of the feelings of anger and offended pride which make us strong in the world's eyes. But this fleshly strength is merely the façade of pride: mere bluster, without any true strength or power behind it.

When we are meek, we display true strength of character: the Christlike character that can bear insults and injustices patiently and silently, trusting God to act in our defense.

Matthew Henry sums this up well:

> *"The more silent we are in our own cause the more is God engaged to plead it. The accused innocent needs to say little if he knows the judge Himself will be his advocate."**

The Christlike response to spiteful words or false accusations is to run to God, trusting that He will not lead us anywhere He is not also ready to defend us.

> "Wherefore let them that suffer according to the will of God commit the keeping of their souls to Him in well doing, as unto a faithful Creator."
> (1 Peter 4:19)

---

*Matthew Henry: *Commentary on the Bible* (Grand Rapids: The Zondervan Corporation 1960) 153

PART 4

They That Hunger and Thirst After Righteousness

7

Beatitude #4: Hunger and Thirst after Righteousness

"Blessed are they which do hunger and thirst after righteousness: for they shall be filled." (Matthew 5:6)

Hunger and Thirst

We all know what it is to experience hunger or thirst, though perhaps not as much as those who gathered on the hillside to hear Jesus speak these words that day. For many of them, hunger and thirst were very serious dangers, indeed.

We acknowledge that hunger and thirst are both recurring sensations that clamor to be filled, but our idea of hungering and thirsting after righteousness often stops short of the idea conveyed here by Jesus.

The Greek word Jesus chose to use for *hunger* has the idea of pinching, or painful, toil to satisfy a need. It can mean to pine, to famish, or to crave.

The idea is that of hunger so serious, so demanding, it must be satisfied immediately. It is a need so urgent you would be willing to do *anything* in order to have it met.

The word for *thirst* here simply means *to thirst*, but it is nevertheless a powerful picture, especially when we bear in mind that this beatitude was first spoken to those who lived in a land where water was precious and thirst a common but deadly danger.

This is the kind of craving we are to have for righteousness. It is an urgent and insistent longing: a need so urgent that we will be willing to do anything it takes to satisfy it. As D. Martyn Lloyd-Jones puts it,

> *"To hunger and thirst really means to be desperate, to be starving, to feel life is ebbing out, to realize my urgent need of help."**

This is a particularly strong sense of urgency indeed, which Jesus uses to describe the Christian's relationship to righteousness.

I wonder… when was the last time you and I felt that kind of urgency to be increasing in righteousness?

After Righteousness

"But," you may ask, "What *is* righteousness?" The word translated *righteousness* here means equity of character or act, specifically of *justification*. It has an implication of holiness, innocence, justice; of being right in the sight of God.

To hunger and thirst after righteousness, then, is to urgently desire to be free from sin, to be right with God. It is to chase after Christ-likeness, not willing to settle for the passive absence of unconfessed sin, but to strive to be *positively* holy, purposely and intentionally working to live out the righteousness of Christ more and more each day.

Filled with Righteousness

Notice the contrast between our deep, urgent, constant need and God's ever-sufficient abundance. When we hunger and thirst for righteousness, we are blessed, or happy, because there is the certainty that we shall be filled.

The Greek word used here for *filled* has an association with the feeding of livestock. The idea is that of providing an animal with an abundant supply of fodder. Jesus is saying here that even our most desperate craving for righteousness can and *will* be fulfilled! There are several aspects to this:

Positional Righteousness

This is what the Bible calls *justification*. It is what happens the moment of salvation when God the Father accepts the blood of Christ as payment for our sins, forgiving our sins and declaring us righteous. The book of Romans deals with this concept of justification. Romans 3:23-26 describes it:

"For all have sinned, and come short of the glory of God; Being justified freely by His grace through the redemption that is in Christ Jesus: Whom God hath set forth to be a propitiation through faith in His blood, to declare His righteousness for the remission of sins that are past, through the forbearance of God; To declare, I say, at this time His righteousness: that He might be just, and the justifier of Him which believeth in Jesus." (3:23-26)

Notice, it is the righteousness of *God* that accomplishes and enables our justification. No righteousness of our own could ever have justified us in the eyes of an all-holy God, but as 1 Corinthians 5:21 explains,

> "He hath made Him to be sin for us, who knew no sin; that we might be made the righteousness of God in Him."

It was Christ's very righteousness that qualified Him to bear our sin, and which now enables the sinner to stand righteous in the sight of God.

Practical Righteousness

While we may be *positionally* righteous before God from the very moment of salvation, we still live with our own sin nature and the temptations of living in a sin-filled world. Scripture is clear that salvation frees us from the power of sin and fills us with the Holy Spirit, which gives us God's power to live in His righteousness. This makes practical holiness a *choice* between serving sin and serving God.

> "But now being made free from sin, and become servants to God, ye have your fruit unto holiness, and the end everlasting life." *(Romans 6:22)*

That choice can be a struggle, however, and Scripture makes equally clear that it is possible for those made righteous through the blood of Christ to fail to live out *practically* the righteousness that is ours *positionally. (Romans 6-7)* When this occurs, we must go back to God for forgiveness and restoration of our relationship with Him.

Of course, this doesn't mean we need to be "re-saved," for salvation is dependent upon the work of Christ on our behalf, not on whether or not we can manage to be "good enough." Salvation brings us out of our position as God's enemies into a new relationship with God: that of children. *(Galatians 4:6; Romans 8:15)*

Sin necessarily strains that relationship with our holy Father, but though that relationship can be strained, it can never be dissolved. (John 10:28)

To restore the relationship, we need to confess our sin (agreeing with God that it *was* sin) and ask forgiveness, just like we would with a family member we have wronged.

1 John 1:9 tells us that,

> "If we confess our sins, He is faithful and just to forgive us our sins, and to cleanse us from all unrighteousness."

Because we have the Holy Spirit indwelling us, the power to say no to sin is always there; we must simply choose to yield to God and access it, for,

> "There hath no temptation taken you but such as is common to man: but God is faithful, who will not suffer you to be tempted above that ye are able; but will with the temptation also make a way to escape, that ye may be able to bear it." (1 Corinthians 10:13)

This practical righteousness is, I think, what Christ had in mind in Matthew 5:6 (if He did not mean all three applications to be made, which is entirely possible.)

As His statement implies, the more we hunger and thirst after righteousness, the more we will be filled, and then hunger for more righteousness, only to be filled again with even more! This craving and being satisfied can go on and on, for in our earthy bodies, the struggle to conquer self and sin is constant.

Promised Righteousness

Of course, this promise that hunger and thirst for righteousness will be satisfied is to be fully and finally manifested upon our entrance into the presence of God, whether at the moment of our death or at the rapture. Then we will be given glorified bodies with no sin nature to battle. Our hunger and thirst for righteousness will be completely and eternally satisfied.

It is no accident that the Greek word used for hunger in Matthew 5:6 is repeated in Revelation 7:16-17, saying of the great multitude worshipping before the throne of God:

"They shall hunger no more, neither thirst any more; neither shall the sun light on them, nor any heat. For the Lamb which is in the midst of the throne shall feed them, and shall lead them unto living fountains of waters: and God shall wipe away all tears from their eyes."

Revelation 21-22 gives another glimpse of what it will be like for us with God throughout eternity.

"And God shall wipe away all tears from their eyes; and there shall be no more death, neither sorrow, nor crying, neither shall there be any more pain: for the former things are passed away."(21:4)

"It is done. I am Alpha and Omega, the beginning and the end. I will give unto him that is athirst of the fountain of the water of life freely." (21:6)

"And the city had no need of the sun, neither of the moon, to shine in it: for the glory of God did lighten it, and the Lamb is the light thereof." (21:23)

"And there shall in no wise enter into it any thing that defileth, neither whatsoever worketh abomination, or maketh a lie: but they which are written in the Lamb's book of life." (21:27)

"And there shall be no more curse: but the throne of God and of the Lamb shall be in it; and His servants shall serve Him: And they shall see His face; and His name shall be in their foreheads. And there shall be no night there; and they need no candle, neither light of the sun; for the Lord God giveth them light: and they shall reign for ever and ever." (22:3-5)

In that bright and blessed eternity, they that hunger and thirst for righteousness shall be perpetually and perfectly filled.

That will be happiness, indeed!

---

*D. Martyn Lloyd-Jones, *Studies in the Sermon on the Mount* (Grand Rapids: Eerdmans 1996) 81

8

David's Hunger and Thirst for Righteousness

When I think of a person in Scripture who exemplified this idea of hungering and thirsting after righteousness, I think of David. Although he was not at all perfect, he nevertheless displayed a heart that longed to do things right: that was willing to fight for righteousness, literally and figuratively, and that mourned when he failed to live out the righteousness he knew God expected of him.

There are several moments throughout David's life where his hunger and thirst for righteousness are clearly displayed. The first is his bold response to Goliath's blasphemous challenge and the Israelite army's blatant fear.

The Philistine army had come to harass Israel and was camped on one side of a valley while the Israelite army camped on the other. In 1 Samuel 17, David sees the army's terrified reaction to Goliath's taunting and asks,

> *"who is this uncircumcised Philistine, that he should*
> *defy the armies of the living God?" (v.26)*

His elder brother, perhaps not wanting to be upstaged, taunted him about his "few sheep in the wilderness," accusing him of coming to the camp just so he could watch the battle. Unabashed, David responds,

> *"What have I now done? Is there not a cause?" (v.29)*

David's confidence in the God of Israel was in sharp contrast to the cringing cowardice of King Saul and his army, and yet David's heart in going to fight Goliath was not to gain fame for himself or showcase his own might or bravery: it was for the sole purpose of showing forth God's might and God's defense of His people. As David said of his defeat of Goliath, it was

> *"That all the earth may know that there is a God in Israel. And all this assembly shall know that the Lord saveth not with sword and spear: for the battle is the Lord's, and he will give you into our hands." (1 Samuel 17:46-47)*

Later on, when David was on the run from the jealous rage of King Saul, he again showed that hunger and thirst for righteousness in his treatment of the very king who had attempted to murder him on multiple occasions and was now hunting him down like a criminal.

When David found himself in the perfect position to kill the man who considered himself David's worst enemy, he would not. Despite the urgings of the group of men he was leading, he would not harm the man God had chosen to be king –even though God had already chosen David to succeed him.

The most David was willing to do was to cut off a small piece of Saul's robe, so he could prove he had been that close to the king. But his conscience was grieved even at that small act. *(1 Samuel 24)*

This firm commitment to do right is seen throughout David's life; and yet, he was not without fault. In the matter of Bathsheba, he sinned grievously, and as he tried to cover up his sin with more sin, his wrongdoing snowballed greater and greater, until Nathan came and declared to David the Lord's message of rebuke and judgment.

I don't know of a passage that speaks more to hungering and thirsting after righteousness than Psalm 51. It was written by David after Nathan's confrontation of his sin. Notice the emphasis on confession and restoration to righteousness.

> "Have mercy upon me, O God, according to Thy lovingkindness: according
> unto the multitude of Thy tender mercies blot out my transgressions.
>
> Wash me thoroughly from mine iniquity, and cleanse me from my sin.
> For I acknowledge my transgressions: and my sin is ever before me.
>
> Against Thee, Thee only, have I sinned, and done this evil in Thy sight:
> that Thou mightest be justified when Thou speakest,
> and be clear when Thou judgest.
>
> Behold, I was shapen in iniquity; and in sin did my mother conceive me.
>
> Behold, Thou desirest truth in the inward parts: and in the
> hidden part Thou shalt make me to know wisdom.
>
> Purge me with hyssop, and I shall be clean:
> wash me, and I shall be whiter than snow.
>
> Make me to hear joy and gladness; that the bones
> which Thou hast broken may rejoice.
>
> Hide Thy face from my sins, and blot out all mine iniquities.

Create in me a clean heart, O God;
and renew a right spirit within me.

Cast me not away from Thy presence; and
take not Thy Holy Spirit from me.

Restore unto me the joy of Thy salvation; and
uphold me with Thy free spirit.

Then will I teach transgressors Thy ways; and
sinners shall be converted unto Thee.

Deliver me from bloodguiltiness, O God, Thou God of my salvation:
and my tongue shall sing aloud of Thy righteousness.

O Lord, open Thou my lips: and my mouth shall shew forth Thy praise.

For Thou desirest not sacrifice; else would I give it:
Thou delightest not in burnt offering.

The sacrifices of God are a broken spirit: a broken and a
contrite heart, O God, Thou wilt not despise.

Do good in Thy good pleasure unto Zion:
build Thou the walls of Jerusalem.

Then shalt Thou be pleased with the sacrifices of righteousness,
with burnt offering and whole burnt offering:
then shall they offer bullocks upon Thine altar."

This psalm is an important part of our understanding of David's hunger and thirst after righteousness. It shows us that we do not have to *begin* in the place of righteousness. Part of hunger and thirst is being fully convinced of our urgent need and our inability to survive unless it is met.

As David faced the reality of his sin, he humbled himself and accepted God's view of the matter, he mourned over his sin, and he yearned to be made right with God: he longed to be righteous and felt the urgency of having his relationship with God restored.

Too often, we skim over the confession of our sins, asking for forgiveness almost flippantly, with no sense of urgency.

A heart that hungers and thirsts for righteousness, *especially* when it has failed, is a heart that will be filled: its cravings fully satisfied with the righteousness of God.

"O God, Thou art my God; early will I seek Thee: my soul thirsteth for Thee, my flesh longeth for Thee in a dry and thirsty land, where no water is." (Psalm 63:1)

PART 5

The Merciful

9

Beatitude #5: The Merciful

"Blessed are the merciful: for they shall obtain mercy."

This beatitude is somewhat self-explanatory. When we show mercy to others, we often, though not always, obtain mercy from them for ourselves. However, in this beatitude, Christ lifts our gaze to a higher level, assuring the merciful that they *shall* receive mercy from God.

The mercy of God is not dependent upon any merit of ours, as Ephesians 2:4-7 reminds us:

"But God, who is rich in mercy, for His great love wherewith he loved us, Even when we were dead in sins, hath quickened us together with Christ, (by grace ye are saved;) And hath raised us up together, and made us sit together in heavenly places in Christ Jesus: That in the ages to come He might shew the exceeding riches of His grace in His kindness toward us through Christ Jesus."

When we were dead in our sins, hopelessly lost and utterly offensive to God, that same God who is perfectly holy and separate from sin, chose to take our sin *on Himself*, that we might be made righteous before Him. *(2 Corinthians 5:21)* That is the richness of God's mercy in action.

From this we can see the kind of mercy Jesus is talking about: mercy that seeks out those who would be unlikely to receive mercy from anyone else, those from whom we expect no kindness in return. Christ did not die so that we would somehow pay back His gift of salvation: His sacrifice was motivated by mercy.

This can be seen in Jesus' teaching in Luke 14:12-14, where He says,

"When thou makest a dinner or a supper, call not thy friends, nor thy brethren, neither thy kinsmen, nor thy rich neighbours; lest they also bid thee again, and a recompence be made thee.

But when thou makest a feast, call the poor, the maimed, the lame, the blind: And thou shalt be blessed; for they cannot recompense thee: for thou shalt be recompensed at the resurrection of the just."

Mercy Defined

The words used in this beatitude for *mercy* and *merciful* also have the idea of compassion. Christ was often noted to have had compassion on various individuals and groups of people throughout the gospels. Yet, while it is certainly biblical to *"Rejoice with them that do rejoice, and weep with them that weep" (Romans 12:15)*. Christ's compassion always motivated Him to act.

Again, Christ's example shows us what our mercy should look like: Christlike mercy is compassion in action.

Mercy does not merely *feel* in accordance with what another is feeling, but also looks around, sees what can be done to help, and quietly does it, without any fanfare or expectation of reward. Mercy is practical compassion, not just emotional compassion.

Another aspect of the mercy of God can be seen in the parable He gave about a remarkably unmerciful servant:

"Therefore is the kingdom of heaven likened unto a certain king, which would take account of his servants. And when he had begun to reckon, one was brought unto him, which owed him ten thousand talents. But forasmuch as he had not to pay, his lord commanded him to be sold, and his wife, and children, and all that he had, and payment to be made. The servant therefore fell down, and worshipped him, saying, Lord, have patience with me, and I will pay thee all. Then the lord of that servant was moved with compassion, and loosed him, and forgave him the debt.

But the same servant went out, and found one of his fellowservants, which owed him an hundred pence: and he laid hands on him, and took him by the throat, saying, Pay me that thou owest. And his fellowservant fell down at his feet, and besought him, saying, Have patience with me, and I will pay thee all. And he would not: but went and cast him into prison, till he should pay the debt.

So when his fellowservants saw what was done, they were very sorry, and came and told unto their lord all that was done. Then his lord, after that he had called him, said unto him, O thou wicked servant, I forgave thee all that debt, because thou desiredst me: Shouldst not thou also have had compassion on thy fellowservant, even as I had pity on thee? And his lord was wroth, and delivered him to the tormentors, till he should pay all that was due unto him.

So likewise shall my heavenly Father do also unto you, if ye from your hearts forgive not every one his brother their trespasses." (Matthew 18:23-35)

We see here the expectation that we should be merciful in forgiving others, just as God in His mercy has forgiven us.

Some would take this passage to mean that if we do not forgive others, God will not forgive us, but that's not exactly what is implied here.

As we have seen already, God's mercy was extended to us *before* we had done anything worthy of His compassion. We were still His enemies, not only unable to pay at that moment but utterly unable to pay the smallest part of our debt of sin.

Add to this that the whole of Scripture clearly teaches that salvation is by grace, not of works, and it is clear that our forgiveness of others cannot have any bearing on our salvation.

The unforgiving servant was not put to the torturers for *eternal* punishment, but only until his debt was paid. Again, that is not how salvation works according to Scripture. Outside of Christ, mankind's punishment for sin is both eternal and inescapable.

When we refuse to forgive, our hearts are not right with God. This results in guilt, hurt, anger, bitterness, and all kinds of spiritual agony which often create physical maladies as well. These torments we cannot escape until we pay the "debt" of forgiveness towards our offender and repentance toward God for our refusal to forgive.

There is also a sense in which the unforgiving Christian, while out of God's will in disobedience to His command to forgive, has stepped out from under God's protection and now stands vulnerable to attack. However, when the unforgiveness is confessed and the choice is made to forgive, God restores the Christian to that place of protection within His good and perfect will.

Our flesh hates to forgive, for forgiveness requires humility. But when we take our eyes off ourselves, forgiveness becomes far easier.

In fact, for the poor in spirit Christian who mourns over his or her own sin and hungers and thirsts after righteousness, meekly allowing God to be the defender, forgiveness will come naturally. It will be the outflowing of a heart aware that its own debt of sin forgiven by God is far greater than any sin he or she may be called upon to forgive in another.

John Wesley describes the merciful as

> "The tender-hearted: They who love all men as themselves." *

This again comes back to the teachings of Jesus:

> "Thou shalt love thy neighbor as thyself" (Matthew 22:39)

> "Therefore all things whatsoever ye would that men should do to you, do ye even so to them: for this is the law and the prophets" (Matthew 7:12)

To be merciful means to extend to others that which God has first extended to us, not only in heartfelt compassion but in forgiveness and selfless action on their behalf. Our mercy should be given freely, just as God's mercy was freely given to us.

---

* *Parallel Commentary on the New Testament.* (Chattanooga: AMG Publishers 2003) p.12

10

The Merciful Stranger

In Luke 10, a man came to Jesus asking, "What shall I do to inherit eternal life?" Jesus replied by asking the man what *he* understood the answer to be, based on what he knew from Scripture. The man replied by summarizing the law, saying,

> "*Thou shalt love the Lord thy God with all thy heart, and with all thy soul, and with all thy strength, and with all thy mind; and thy neighbour as thyself.*" (v.25)

Jesus agreed with this summary, saying,

> "*This do, and thou shalt live,*" (v.28)

But that answer did not satisfy the man. Scripture tells us that the man, seeking to justify himself, asked for further clarification.

> "*Who is my neighbour?*" (v.29)

Knowing that the man's goal was only to excuse his own lack of compassion, Jesus illustrated with the following parable:

"A certain man went down from Jerusalem to Jericho, and fell among thieves, which stripped him of his raiment, and wounded him, and departed, leaving him half dead. And by chance there came down a certain priest that way: and when he saw him, he passed by on the other side. And likewise a Levite, when he was at the place, came and looked on him, and passed by on the other side.

But a certain Samaritan, as he journeyed, came where he was: and when he saw him, he had compassion on him, And went to him, and bound up his wounds, pouring in oil and wine, and set him on his own beast, and brought him to an inn, and took care of him.

And on the morrow when he departed, he took out two pence, and gave them to the host, and said unto him, Take care of him; and whatsoever thou spendest more, when I come again, I will repay thee.

Which now of these three, thinkest thou, was neighbour unto him that fell among the thieves?"(vv.30-36)

I don't know what the man thought or how he felt about Jesus' story, but he gave the right answer:

"He that showed mercy on him."(v.37)

It is easy to read this story and cheer for the good Samaritan, making much of his character and generosity, but miss the practical application of what Jesus intended it to illustrate.

Of the three men who traveled that road and saw the wounded man, the Samaritan was not the most likely to stop. In fact, to the Jewish audience to which Jesus spoke this parable, Samaritans were considered apostate half-breeds, hated and despised.

Great lengths were taken by the Jews of Jesus' day to avoid traveling through Samaria to get anywhere else, and the mere mention of a Samaritan in Jesus' parable likely shocked some of His hearers, let alone the Samaritan appearing in the role of the hero.

For the *Samaritan* of all people to show mercy to the Jewish man would have been a surprising plot twist, especially since the hatred between the Jews and the Samaritans was not at all one-sided.

It is interesting how Jesus chose to phrase this parable: it is a *certain man*, a specific road, a *certain priest*, a *certain Samaritan*: all this makes it quite likely that Jesus is relating something that had actually happened. In fact, one commentator I read suggested that this may have been an event of which some in the crowd would have had personal knowledge.

That is all just interesting speculation, but it does seem from what Jesus said that this was no made-up story, but rather a real-life illustration of what it means to be merciful.

It is often pointed out (and rightly so) that the Samaritan didn't let the man's heritage stop him from showing mercy on the wounded man. In our current culture, I think it is needful to also mention that the Samaritan also did not let the wounded man's feelings towards *his* heritage stop him. There was no excuse of "I can't help him, he's a Jew. They hate us!" The man needed help, so the Samaritan helped him.

The Samaritan's example is a good reminder to us that we are to show mercy to others regardless of who they are, what society thinks of them —or even what they think about us. After all, God Himself showed us mercy while we were still at enmity with Him.

> "But God commendeth His love toward us, in that, while we were yet sinners, Christ died for us." (Romans 5:8)

The knowledge of how much mercy God has extended to you and me ought to give us hearts that are ready, willing, even eager to pour our own pitiful store of mercy out on others. When the Holy Spirit prompts us to some act or word or service of mercy, let us obey immediately, regardless of that person's personality, beliefs, past actions, or attitude towards us. God's mercy extends to the lowest and the least –and aren't you glad it extended to you?

PART 6

The Pure in Heart

11

Beatitude #6: Pure in Heart

"Blessed are the pure in heart: for they shall see God."
Matthew 5:8

Like mercy, purity of heart is a direct result of the poor-in-spirit Christian seeing sin as God sees it. That Christian will mourn over his or her own sin, meekly accepting God's standard of righteousness, and hungering to meet it with all the intensity of the most urgent need. This will necessarily bring us into closer fellowship with God, which will purify our hearts.

To be *pure* means to be clean or clear, figuratively or literally. To have a pure heart is not only to have a heart that is cleansed from sin, as at salvation, but also a heart that desires to *stay* clean before God.

Just like a clean floor needs regular attention if it is to stay clean, our hearts need that ongoing confession of sin and restoration of fellowship as we live as saved, yet still sinners, in the midst of a filthy world. This side of heaven, purity of heart requires a constant battle against the world, the flesh, and the devil.

As with the other beatitudes, this is a fairly simple concept, but not at all easy to put into practice. Yet, purity of heart is at the very center of Christianity. After all, the point of salvation is that we need our hearts cleansed from sin, and of course, what Christ has cleansed we should naturally desire to keep clean.

Consider what 1Timothy 1:5 says,

> *"Now the end of the commandment is charity out of a pure heart, and of a good conscience, and of faith unfeigned"*

Our love for others, our mercy, our meekness, and every other aspect of our interactions with others flows from our hearts. A pure heart will value others the way God values them and will treat them accordingly. However, if our hearts are soiled by the grime of unconfessed sin, we will treat others according to the selfishness and deceitfulness of our old sin nature.

Purity of heart strikes me as a single-minded focus. Jesus Himself mentions later in this same "Sermon on the Mount,"

> *"The light of the body is the eye: if therefore thine eye be single, thy whole body shall be full of light. But if thine eye be evil, thy whole body shall be full of darkness. If therefore the light that is in thee be darkness, how great is that darkness!" (Matthew 6:22-23)*

Our eyes determine our focus. When we keep our eyes set on the world and worldly things, our focus will be worldly, and the light of Christ which ought to shine through us to the benighted world around will be dimmed more and more as we embrace the world's darkness. But when we set our gaze on the things of God, our light grows brighter and brighter. The purer our hearts, the brighter our light. Paul says,

> "Brethren, I count not myself to have apprehended: but this one thing I do, forgetting those things which are behind, and reaching forth unto those things which are before, I press toward the mark for the prize of the high calling of God in Christ Jesus." (Philippians 3:13-14)

His one goal, the one thing for which he worked and longed, was *"The high calling of God in Christ Jesus."* When we become Christians, we are called to be ambassadors. (2 Corinthians 5:20) Jesus Himself said, just a few verses away from the beatitudes,

> "Ye are the light of the world. A city that is set on an hill cannot be hid. Neither do men light a candle, and put it under a bushel, but on a candlestick; and it giveth light unto all that are in the house. Let your light so shine before men, that they may see your good works, and glorify your Father which is in heaven." (Matthew 5:14-16)

Purity of heart will always lead us towards the fulfillment of our calling to be lights, examples, and beacons of hope and righteousness that will lead others to the one in Whom there is no darkness at all. (1 John 1:5) Purity of heart also leads to a glorious result:

> *"for they shall see God."* (Matthew 5:8)

Matthew Henry explains this well:

> "None but the pure are capable of seeing God, nor would heaven be happiness to the impure. As God cannot endure to look upon their iniquity, so they cannot look upon His purity." *

You see, when our hearts are made pure before God at salvation, we are given the unfailingly certain promise that we will see Him one day, face to face. (1 Corinthians 13:12)

In the glorious description of eternity ahead with God in the New Jerusalem, we are told,

"And there shall be no more curse: but the throne of God and of the Lamb shall be in it; and His servants shall serve Him: And they shall see His face..." (Revelation 22:3-4)

But, as with so many of the other promises made in these beatitudes, there is an earthly aspect to the promise as well as the obvious heavenly fulfillment. This is seen in 1 John 3:2-3.

"Beloved, now are we the sons of God, and it doth not yet appear what we shall be: but we know that, when He shall appear, we shall be like Him; for we shall see Him as He is. And every man that hath this hope in him purifieth himself, even as He is pure."

The knowledge that we will one day see God face to face, in the indescribable glory of all that He is, serves as motivation to purify ourselves *now*, while we wait for His coming. And notice, too, that beholding God makes us become more like Him. 2 Corinthians puts it this way:

"But we all, with open face beholding as in a glass the glory of the Lord, are changed into that same image from glory to glory, even as by the Spirit of the Lord." (3:18)

Here on earth, we wait for that sweet someday when we will see God face to face and be given new bodies, pure and free from our sin natures. But while we wait, we strive to become more and more like God as we catch more and more glimpses of His glory.

So how do we get there? How do we develop that single-minded striving to keep our hearts pure before God?

Psalm 119 gives us the answer:

"Wherewithal shall a young man cleanse his way? by taking heed thereto according to Thy Word. With my whole heart have I sought Thee: O let me not wander from Thy commandments. Thy Word have I hid in mine heart, that I might not sin against Thee." (vv.9-11)

Purity of heart begins with God's Word. One of the things Jesus prayed for His disciples in John 17 was,

"Sanctify them through Thy truth: Thy Word is truth." (v.17)

He then went on to say that He prayed this not just for His disciples, but also for *all* those who would believe in Him through their word (i.e., you and me.)

We are sanctified, or set apart *from* sin and *to* God, through the Scripture. This means that the way we grow in striving after purity of heart is to immerse ourselves in God's Word, saturating our thinking with His truth. That is exactly what the author of Psalm 119 did. It is where his heart to study, learn, obey, and delight in God's Word came from.

When I was a teen, my brother came home from Bible college with a grand plan to memorize Psalm 119—and for me to memorize it along with him! Now, I hadn't memorized any verses since I grew too old for Vacation Bible School, and Psalm 119 happens to be the very *longest* chapter in the entire Bible, but I loved my brother and respected his zeal to be learning and memorizing Scripture, so I went along with it.

I don't remember exactly how far he got, but I know that *I* only got through 56 verses before we both lost momentum and eventually gave up. Even though I didn't accomplish the outward goal of memorizing all 176 verses, the inward goal God had in mind for me *was* accomplished.

You see, memorizing such a lengthy passage meant *time*. I read each stanza over and over: on the bus, in the car, walking to and from different places; I carried my Bible with me always, so that I could use every spare moment to work on memorizing the psalm.

To be honest, I had begun memorizing the psalm to please my brother. However, the more time I spent reading, repeating, and reviewing the verses, the more truth I noticed in them, and the more *I* grew to share the love the unnamed psalmist had for God's Word. The verses resonated with where I *was* in my Christian growth, as well as where I *wanted* to be.

I didn't realize it at the time, but that memorization project would be a defining force in my growth towards a greater measure of spiritual maturity. It was the Holy Spirit of God quickening the Word of God to my heart that developed within me the desire, the longing, the thirst for holiness that still motivates me to strive after purity of heart.

And if you come to it honestly, with a poor in spirit heart, humbly submissive to its truths, that's exactly what the Word of God will do for *you*.

> *"Behold, I have longed after Thy precepts:*
> *quicken me in Thy righteousness." (Psalm 119:40)*

---

*Parallel Commentary on the New Testament. (Chattanooga: AMG Publishers 2003) p. 15

12

Pure Heart in a Pagan Land

Daniel is indisputably one of the great heroes of the faith. Even if you aren't a student of the Bible, you probably have at least a few vague memories of references to Daniel in the lion's den.

God Himself refers to Daniel in the book of Ezekiel three times, twice declaring of Jerusalem,

> "Though these three men, Noah, Daniel, and Job, were in it, they should deliver but their own souls by their righteousness, saith the Lord God."
> (Ezekiel 14:14,20)

Later on in Ezekiel, God again mentions Daniel, saying derisively to the prideful prince of Tyrus,

> "Behold, thou art wiser than Daniel; there is no secret that they can hide from thee" (Ezekiel 28:3)

This shows that Daniel was well known for his wisdom and for his righteousness throughout the Babylonian empire.

The book of Daniel records many instances of Daniel standing up for righteousness, whatever the cost. But all that didn't just happen. It began with a decision.

Daniel was taken captive in the first Babylonian siege of Jerusalem in 605 BC. *(2 Kings 24:1-2)* He was apparently either from the royal family or else one of the leading families of Judah, and so was chosen in response to Nebuchadnezzar's command to bring to Babylon,

"Children in whom was no blemish, but well-favoured, and skilful in all wisdom, and cunning in knowledge, and understanding science, and such as had ability in them to stand in the king's palace, and whom they might teach the learning and the tongue of the Chaldeans." (Daniel 1:4)

This long list of accomplishments tells us what kind of education and looks Daniel had, but it isn't until verse 8 that we find out what kind of heart he had.

The king was generous with the new arrivals, giving them meat and wine from his own table, and giving them three years to "catch up" with their Babylonian training before being brought into the kings' presence.

But there was a problem. The food so generously provided to the captives was defiling in the eyes of the Judean captives, who had apparently been brought up to follow the law despite the general rebellion of their society as a whole.

What could they do? They were far away from home, and no one in Babylon was likely to care about the religious beliefs of a few prisoners. To refuse anything the king commanded, especially for religious reasons was extremely dangerous, and could even be fatal since the Babylonian kings were at times worshipped as deities.

The captives had no rights, no way to make their captors understand the importance of adherence to God's laws. Even to attempt it must have seemed foolish and futile. This is the situation in which we find Daniel in verse 8.

"But Daniel purposed in his heart that he would not defile himself with the portion of the king's meat, nor with the wine which he drank"

This is the beginning of the amazing and miraculous things God did for and through Daniel. Not only did the man in charge of him listen to his appeal, the proposed "experiment" of eating only the part of the king's food that would not defile them was widely successful.

It is easy to look at a man like Daniel and think that it was somehow just easier for him to stand up for righteousness. But Daniel wasn't just naturally a "better person" than the rest of us: he simply made a choice to focus on doing right, whatever the cost.

His heart was set on following God; and that pure focus of heart helped him to stay strong against peer pressure *(Daniel 1)*, against the intimidation of a prideful king *(Daniel 2-4)*, against the offer of a wicked ruler's wealth *(Daniel 5:16-17)*, and even against the threat of a gruesome death *(Daniel 6)*.

Whatever test came Daniel's way, he passed it, not because he was perfect, but because he had a pure heart committed to obeying God.

Purity of heart is rare, because our hearts are naturally *"deceitful above all things, and desperately wicked." (Jeremiah 17:9)* To get our hearts pure, we simply confess our sin and ask for forgiveness. Then we strive to keep our hearts pure, going to God immediately when we sin, knowing that He is *faithful and just to forgive us our sins, and to cleanse us from all unrighteousness" (1 John 1:9)* The closer our relationship to God, the purer our hearts will be.

After the final destruction of Jerusalem, the prophet Jeremiah wrote to the captives in Babylon with a message from God. I wonder if Daniel found comfort, strength, and encouragement in these words then, as I do today:

"For I know the thoughts that I think toward you, saith the Lord, thoughts of peace, and not of evil, to give you an expected end. Then shall ye call upon Me, and ye shall go and pray unto Me, and I will hearken unto you. And ye shall seek Me, and find Me, when ye shall search for Me with all your heart." (Jeremiah 29:11-13)

PART 7

The Peacemakers

13

Beatitude #7: Peacemakers

"Blessed are the peacemakers: for they shall be called the children of God." (Matthew 5:9)

We humans are not naturally creatures of peace. We argue, we fight, and we fuss and fume if we don't get our way. We are selfish, and our selfishness is the exact opposite of what it means to be a peacemaker.

It is common to think of a peacemaker as a naturally easygoing, peace-at-all-costs sort of person who has a dread of conflict and thus attempts to please everyone. That might be what the world would say a peacemaker is, but it is not the Biblical definition of a peacemaker.

The word translated *peacemaker* in this verse is simply the form of the word for *peace* that gives the sense of making or doing. It implies an active effort to make peace, by doing things that will make peace.

While the English word *peacemaker* only occurs just this once in the Bible, the Greek word appears in the same form several other places as well, each giving us a glimpse into what it means to be a peacemaker.

Peace with the Wrongdoer

Romans 12:18-21 shows us what it means to be a peacemaker when we personally have been wronged:

"If it be possible, as much as lieth in you, live peaceably with all men. Dearly beloved, avenge not yourselves, but rather give place unto wrath: for it is written, Vengeance is Mine, I will repay, saith the Lord. Therefore if thine enemy hunger, feed him; if he thirst, give him drink: for in so doing thou shalt heap coals of fire on his head. Be not overcome of evil, but overcome evil with good."

This passage tells us that the Christian is not to pursue vengeance or seek to take the punishment of the wicked into his or her own hands. Instead, we are to actively seek to do good to those who have wronged us, diligently finding out their needs and meeting them to the best of our ability. That is being a peacemaker.

Of course, this does not abolish the proper administration of justice: it simply means that the Christian, when wronged, can rest in the knowledge that God's ultimate justice *will* be done in His timing.

In the case of wrongdoing that has violated society's laws, Scripture makes it clear that it is proper for the Christian to expect society to administer justice.

The emphasis here is not that wrongdoing should never be punished, but rather that we are to leave that punishment to the proper authority in the knowledge that, whether or not earthly authorities are willing or able to bring the wrongdoer to justice, God is the Judge of all. He will make it right in His timing.

1 Peter 4:19 says,

> "Wherefore let them that suffer according to the will of God commit the keeping of their souls to Him in well doing, as unto a faithful Creator."

We can be peacemakers even to those who have done us or our loved ones wrong, because we can trust the faithfulness of our Creator that has forgiven our own wrongdoing towards Himself.

Peace with our Surroundings

> "Finally brethren, farewell. Be perfect, be of good comfort, be of one mind, live in peace; and the God of love and peace shall be with you." (2 Corinthians 13:11)

This verse reminds me that to live in peace, we must humbly accept the people and circumstances God has placed in our lives. We cannot make peace with those around us if we do not first have peace in ourselves!

Often, one of the things that hinder us from being the peacemakers God desires us to be is bitterness about some aspect of our life. We know God has allowed it and plans to use it for our good; but we can't quite bring ourselves to accept it or believe that it could be turned into anything good.

Look at 2 Corinthians 13:11 again and notice the things Paul told the Corinthians to do. Each one takes humility, either before God or our fellow Christians. Living in peace takes humility as well. Those things in our lives over which we are fuming or fretting keep us from living in peace with God and with others.

It is pride and selfishness that says to God, "I don't like that part of my life, and I *won't* be happy while it exists, so *there!*"

Until we bring those things to God, humbly confessing our pride and selfishness in surrender to His will, we will never get our focus off ourselves long enough to do anything to aid the peace of anyone else. To be a peacemaker is to reject our natural selfishness and live with our focus on others.

Peace with our Fellow Christians

This brings us to the third passage: this time the word *peacemaker* is translated *"at peace."*

"And we beseech you, brethren, to know them which labour among you, and are over you in the Lord, and admonish you; And to esteem them very highly in love for their work's sake. And be at peace among yourselves." (1 Thessalonians 5:12-13)

This reminds us that we are to be a peacemaker within the church. Romans 12 tells us that the church is the body of Christ, made up of many members, with many different functions. We are, however, still sinners, saved by grace but still struggling with a sin nature.

That is why it is so vital that Christians be peacemakers. As members of the body of Christ, our purpose is to serve God. We must lay aside our selfishness, rejecting the "right" to hold grudges or demand attention. We must speak that which will edify, or build up, instead of that which will tear down. We must seek to live and act and react to life the way Jesus would. If we all did that, we would truly be at peace among ourselves!

D. Martyn Lloyd-Jones described the peacemaker as:

> *"the man whose central concern is the glory of God, and who spends his life in trying to minister to that glory."* *

To keep our eyes and hearts focused on God's glory is to live in readiness to be a peacemaker. Of course, the ultimate way we can further peace is to share the gospel, for it is through Christ that we have peace with God. *(Romans 5:1)*

We can be peacemakers with those who have wronged us by actively looking for ways to do them good, as Christ did for us. And we can be peacemakers within the church by setting self aside and looking for ways to encourage and edify our brothers and sisters in Christ.

Children of God

The promise of this beatitude is that peacemakers will be called the children of God. 1 John 3:1 says,

> *"Behold, what manner of love the Father hath bestowed upon us, that we should be called the sons of God: therefore the world knoweth us not, because it knew Him not."*

When we live as peacemakers in this world, we display our "family resemblance" to God, who has called us His own children. The world doesn't recognize a peacemaker. It thinks it strange and abnormal for someone to do good to their enemies with a sincere heart. It cannot understand why anyone would "put up with" the things a peacemaker chooses to overlook, or why that peacemaker will not take vengeance on one who has wronged him or her when the opportunity arises.

We may have the world's approval for a while, insomuch as our peacemaking efforts comprise just generally being a "nice person;" but there is a reason Romans 12:18 begins with the words, *"If it be possible."*

The world is no champion of true peace. It is too much a fan of its own selfishness to applaud the selfless for very long. Yet, regardless of how the world perceives us, to be called the children of God should be our greatest joy, and the furtherance of His glory our greatest desire.

*D. Martyn Lloyd-Jones, *Studies in the Sermon on the Mount*. Grand Rapids: Eerdmans.1996 p. 123

14

A Powerful Peacemaker

The life of Joseph is an incredible example of God's grace at work in the heart of a man who chose to forgive, though he had been horribly wronged.

You might not think of Joseph as a peacemaker, but throughout his life, there is not one recorded instance of him seeking revenge. Instead, he actively worked to do good to those who wronged him.

Joseph was clearly his father Jacob's favorite son, and his brothers hated him from a young age. Eventually, they threw him in a pit; and when the opportunity arose to sell him to slave traders from Egypt, they readily agreed.

They covered up what they had done by telling their father that Joseph had been killed by wild beasts. Then, apart from Jacob's grief over his son, life in Canaan just went right on without Joseph. That is, until the famine came.

Food began to dwindle; and when Joseph's father Jacob heard that there was food in the land of Egypt, he decided to send ten of his remaining sons. Little did they know that they were about to come face to face with their long-lost brother.

They didn't recognize him, of course. So many years had passed, and now he was dressed as a high-ranking Egyptian. They would never have imagined that the brother they so hated and sold as a slave had risen to become the second most powerful man in all Egypt! Imagine their grave surprise, shock, and terror when Joseph finally revealed his identity.

And yet, though Joseph first tested his brothers to ascertain the state of their hearts, he had already shown himself generous and eager to help his family survive the famine. Not only that, but when he had opportunity to berate them for the wrong they had done him, he pointed them instead to the truth that God had used it for good. Here is what he said:

> *"Now therefore be not grieved, nor angry with yourselves, that ye sold me hither: for God did send me before you to preserve life." (Genesis 45:5)*

He then assured them that he would take care of them through the five remaining years of famine. Not only did he show them his heart of forgiveness and his faith-filled perspective on the events of their past, he also made peace with them by offering to meet their physical needs.

Later on, their father died, and the brothers again feared that Joseph would exact revenge. After all, he was the most powerful man in Egypt, except for Pharaoh, and could have punished them in whatever way he chose.

They sent off a hurried message saying that their father made it his dying wish that Joseph would forgive them, then appeared before him themselves, bowing to the ground in humility. Joseph replied:

"Fear not: for am I in the place of God? But as for you, ye thought evil against me; but God meant it unto good, to bring to pass, as it is this day, to save much people alive. Now therefore fear ye not: I will nourish you, and your little ones." (Genesis 50:19-21)

Joseph was able to promote his brother's peace by extending his full and free forgiveness for their wrong. Though he was powerful, he was a peacemaker. He chose to see his brothers as God saw them, and to see their wrongdoing from the vantage point of the great good which God had chosen to bring out of it.

The foundation of being a peacemaker like Joseph is the willingness to set aside grievances and offenses, focusing instead on God and resting in the good He can bring out of even the worst situations.

> *"And we know that all things work together for good to them that love God, to them who are the called according to His purpose." (Romans 8:28)*

PART 8

Persecuted for Righteousness

15

Beatitude #8 Persecuted

"Blessed are they which are persecuted for righteousness' sake: for theirs is the kingdom of heaven." (Matthew 5:10)

This beatitude seems on the surface like an extreme contradiction. After all, who would be happy to be persecuted? And yet, "happy" is just what the word "blessed" literally means.

Perhaps this paradox will be easier to unravel if we consider the fact that it is not the persecution itself that makes us happy, but the *cause* for which we are persecuted.

For Righteousness' Sake

The blessedness of persecution hinges on the fact that we are not being persecuted because of something wrong we have done. I Peter 4:14-15 gives us the most concise explanation of this concept:

"*If ye be reproached for the name of Christ, happy are ye; for the Spirit of glory and of God resteth upon you: on their part He is evil spoken of, but on your part He is glorified. But let none of you suffer as a murderer, or as a thief, or as an evildoer, or as a busybody in other men's matters. Yet if any man suffer as a Christian, let him not be ashamed; but let him glorify God on this behalf.*"

Persecution for righteousness' sake comes for the simple reason that we are *like* Christ and *unlike* the world. It is the natural consequence of exhibiting the Christlike character of all the preceding beatitudes, for the righteousness of Christ makes all the world's self-righteousness look decidedly shabby.

The more we grow in the righteousness of Christ, the more the world hates us, because the world hates Christ. As Jesus said,

"*If the world hate you, ye know that it hated Me before it hated you. If ye were of the world, the world would love his own: but because ye are not of the world, but I have chosen you out of the world, therefore the world hateth you.*" (John 15:18-19)

I love the way D. Martyn Lloyd-Jones puts this:

"To become like Him we have to become light; light always exposes darkness, and the darkness therefore always hates the light."*

Our growth in righteousness will inevitably bring us into the way of persecution of some form. It may be as mild as looks of contempt or spiteful words, or it may even be as extreme as martyrdom. God has a unique plan for each of His children, but one common thread runs through them all:

> *"In the world ye shall have tribulation: but be of good cheer;*
> *I have overcome the world." (John 16:33)*

To suffer for righteousness' sake is part of following Christ. In fact, the early Christians considered it to be the greatest honor. In Acts 5, the apostles, having just been beaten for preaching the gospel,

> *"departed from the presence of the council, rejoicing that they were counted worthy to suffer shame for His name." (Acts 5:41)*

We cannot avoid conflict with the world: but we can make sure that the conflict is due to the righteousness of Christ shining through us and not our own sinful attitudes and actions. If the world is persecuting us because we are living righteously, we can be encouraged to know that we are following in the footsteps of Christ.

> *"For even hereunto were ye called: because Christ also suffered for us, leaving us an example, that ye should follow His steps: Who did no sin, neither was guile found in His mouth: Who, when He was reviled, reviled not again; when He suffered, He threatened not; but committed Himself to Him that judgeth righteously: Who His own self bare our sins in His own body on the tree, that we, being dead to sins, should live unto righteousness: by whose stripes ye were healed." (1 Peter 2:21-24)*

Theirs is the Kingdom of Heaven

As much encouragement as we can find in the occurrence of persecution which arises because we are growing in Christlikeness, there is even more encouragement to be found in the precious promise tied to persecution throughout Scripture: that the suffering of the persecuted Christian is never unrewarded.

The word for persecution in Matthew 5 has the idea of being pursued or pressed forward. Thus, there is a great contrast in this beatitude. To those whom the world has hunted down and driven from place to place, it promises a future of ownership in the very kingdom of heaven.

They may be poor and persecuted now, but in the kingdom of God they will be rulers, for the Christian who suffers for Christ will one day reign with Him. *(2 Timothy 2:11-12)*

A few verses after this promise about the kingdom of heaven, Jesus says we ought to respond to persecution this way:

"Rejoice, and be exceeding glad, for great is your reward in heaven"
(Matthew 5:12)

The point is not to rejoice in the physical or emotional pain of persecution, but rather to glory in its cause and its future result.

We rejoice in persecution because it shows that we are in some measure reflecting the righteousness of Christ; and we rejoice in persecution because we know with the utmost certainty that God is a righteous Judge, and that He will one day correct the injustice of our persecution and reward us for enduring it faithfully. We can rest in the truth of Romans 8:35-39.

"Who shall separate us from the love of Christ? Shall tribulation, or distress, or persecution, or famine, or nakedness, or peril, or sword? As it is written, For Thy sake we are killed all the day long; we are accounted as sheep for the slaughter. Nay, in all these things we are more than conquerors through Him that loved us. For I am persuaded, that neither death, nor life, for angels, nor principalities, nor powers, nor things present, nor things to come, Nor height, nor depth, nor any other creature, shall be able to separate us from the love of God, which is in Christ Jesus our Lord."

*D. Martyn Lloyd-Jones, *Studies in the Sermon on the Mount* (Grand Rapids: Eerdmans 1996) p. 137

16

Blessed Are Ye

"Blessed are ye, when men shall revile you, and persecute you, and shall say all manner of evil against you falsely, for My sake. Rejoice, and be exceeding glad: for great is your reward in heaven: for so persecuted they the prophets which were before you." (Matthew 5:11-12)

This final beatitude (which is sometimes counted as part of the one before it) brings the truths of these statements from theoretical to practical. It reminds us that these statements are not just lofty truths to be assented to in our heads, but that they are statements of practical truth: meant to be *lived*, not just pondered.

Nor is it just the super-Christian for whom these blessings are meant: they are for you and me, as we submit to God's view of us and our sin, yield to the Holy Spirit's promptings and thus grow in righteousness. We are those whom Christ had in mind when He spoke these things, for He wants us to *"grow in grace and in the knowledge of our Lord Jesus Christ" (2 Peter 3:18)*

I believe that is why Jesus chose this abrupt turn of phrase: to show us that He isn't speaking of some theoretical individual that may or may not exist, but to us personally.

We are to live in such a way that the world hates us for our resemblance to Christ. We are to expect persecution, and to weather it with rejoicing in the rewards it will occasion in heaven to come. The beatitudes are not simply to be enjoyed as beautiful words: they are faithful promises to which we can cling when the going gets rough.

It is difficult to end this study here, for with the statement of *"Blessed are ye"* Christ's sermon takes off into many practical truths and Divine maxims. To do justice to the rest of the Sermon on the Mount would be a much longer study, so end here I must.

And yet, I think it is important to leave us with a picture of what we will become to the world if we live in light of these beatitudes:

"Ye are the salt of the earth: but if the salt have lost his savour, wherewith shall it be salted? It is thenceforth good for nothing, but to be cast out, and to be trodden under foot of men. Ye are the light of the world. A city that is on a hill cannot be hid. Neither do men light a candle, and put it under a bushel, but on a candlestick, and it giveth light to all that are in the house. Let your light so shine before men, that they may see your good works and glorify your Father which is in heaven." (Matthew 5:13-16)

When we live out the truths of Christ's statements, when we show to the world what it means to be poor in spirit, to mourn over our sin, to live in meekness, to hunger and thirst after righteousness, to extend mercy to others, to walk in pureness of heart, to be peacemakers, and to endure persecution with Christlike humility and joy: then we will be the lights Christ described in the verses above.

When we live as reflections of the light of Christ, the world will rage, mock, revile, and persecute; but our light, while exposing the world's darkness for what it is, will also draw some to its Source. For to be salt in a saltless world, light in utter darkness: that is to be our purpose and our joy.

"For ye were sometimes darkness, but now are ye light in the Lord: walk as children of light" (Ephesians 5:8)

www.ingramcontent.com/pod-product-compliance
Lightning Source LLC
Chambersburg PA
CBHW070937080526
44589CB00013B/1545